T0005488

Ernő Rubik
AND HIS MAGIC
CUBE

3 and turn 3

WRITTEN BY
KERRY ARADHYA

Ω
PEACHTREE
ATLANTA

ILLUSTRATED BY
KARA KRAMER

use these puzzles as a starting point to dis cover

In the hills of Budapest, near the banks of the Danube River, lived a quiet boy named Ernő.

While other children played outside his flat, Ernő preferred to be alone.

But Ernő didn't *feel* alone.

He was with his books.

He was with his pencils.

And he was with his favorite playmates of all:

his puzzles.

Ernő was curious about the
objects around him.

What did they look like on the inside?

Drawing them helped him understand the world.

He was also curious about geometric shapes.

How many ways could he fit them together?

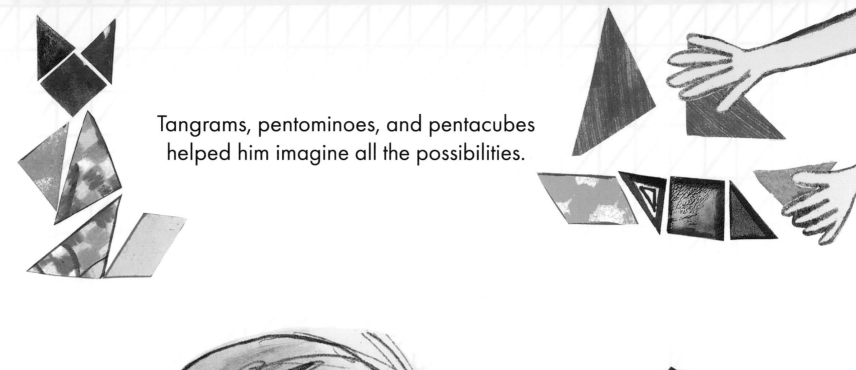

Tangrams, pentominoes, and pentacubes helped him imagine all the possibilities.

Ernő thought the three-dimensional objects he created out of his little cubes were beautiful.

Ernő thought nature was beautiful, too.

Every summer he traveled to Lake Balaton
with his family. The warm air, clear water,
and swaying of wild reeds along the shore
inspired him.

So did the days and nights he spent sailing
the lake in peaceful solitude.

As the summers
passed . . .

Ernő studied art.

He studied architecture.

He became a teacher.

Ernő built models to teach his students about three-dimensional objects. He was most curious about cubes. He wondered . . .

Would it be possible to build a big cube out of smaller cubes that moved around each other *and* stayed connected?

He decided to try it!

8 cubes

To make the big cube, Ernő cut eight little cubes out of wood and drilled a hole in the corner of each one.

He used rubber bands and paper clips to join them together.

But the big cube fell

He tried fishing line.

But the cube crumbled again.

Ernő was determined to figure out this puzzle!

He started over.

This time he cut twenty-seven
little cubes out of wood.

He arranged them in three rows of three . . .

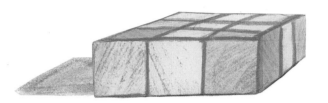

then three rows of three on top of those . . .

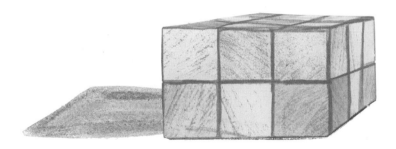

and then three rows of three on top of those.

Then he removed the little cube in the center. The others
would move around each other better that way.

But he still needed something stronger than rubber bands
or fishing line to hold them together.

What could that *something* be?

Ernő thought about it for one day.

He thought about it for two days.

And many days later, when
he had stopped thinking
about it, he went for a walk.

Ernő wandered the busy streets of Budapest
and made his way to the banks of the Danube.

Like the summer lake from his childhood, the river was peaceful.

As he walked along the water, Ernő noticed how easily it moved
around the smooth, round pebbles that dotted the shore.

IF YOU ARE

SOLVE THEM

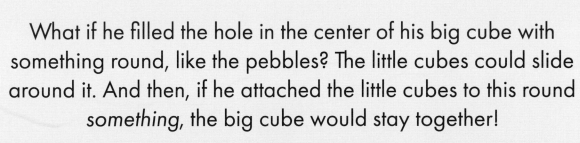
What if he filled the hole in the center of his big cube with something round, like the pebbles? The little cubes could slide around it. And then, if he attached the little cubes to this round *something*, the big cube would stay together!

His heart pounded faster than his feet against the cobblestone.

Ernő sketched . . .

cut . . .

sanded.

Ernő drilled . . .

screwed . . .

assembled.

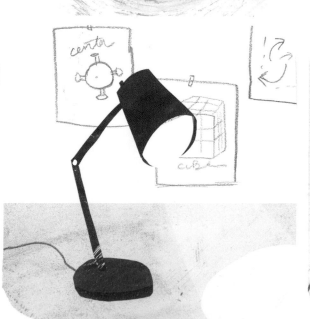

One last touch . . .

And Ernő's cube, made of twenty-six little cubes and one round mechanical core, was complete.

Ernő thought the three-dimensional object he had created was beautiful.

As he twisted and turned, a parade of colors
—yellow, orange, green, blue, red, white—
danced between his fingers.

It was pure . . . MAGIC!

He didn't know it yet, but in solving one puzzle for himself, twenty-nine-year-old Ernő Rubik had unexpectedly invented another one for the world.

In the years to come, more than a billion people would hold his magic cube . . .

twisting and turning . . .

turning and twisting . . .

Trying to solve the most popular
puzzle in history.

43,252,003,274,489,856,000

The Magic Cube

If you think Ernő Rubik knew how to solve the puzzle he'd invented, you'd be wrong. That's because he never intended to invent a puzzle at all! It was only after twisting and turning the three-dimensional object, and losing track of its original position, that he became curious about how to restore order to the chaos he'd created.

Today you can find books, websites, and videos to help you solve the Cube. But back then, in the spring of 1974, Rubik was on his own. It took him about a month to find a solution, and he did it using a combination of intuition and logic. He named the puzzle Bűvös Kocka, or the Magic Cube, and it was released in Hungary before being rebranded as the Rubik's Cube.

Ernő Rubik designed other puzzles such as the Snake (now known as Rubik's Twist) and Rubik's Magic, but none became as popular as his Cube. Despite the attention he received for his invention, Rubik preferred to maintain a quiet life. When this book was written, he was still living in his hometown of Budapest, continuing to design, teach, and support students of all ages in the art and science of problem-solving.

By the Numbers

1 Rubik's Cube = **1** mechanical core + **26** little cubes called "cubies"
26 cubies = **6** center cubies + **8** corner cubies + **12** edge cubies

1 Rubik's Cube = **6** sides
6 sides x **4** positions in space when any side faces up = **24** positions in space
6 sides x **9** stickers on each side = **54** stickers

43 quintillion ways to scramble it . . . but only **1** solution!

In 2010, Google donated computer time to researchers who wanted to determine what is called God's Number—the smallest number of moves needed to solve a Cube from any of the **43,252,003,274,489,856,000** possible starting positions. It took **35** computer processing unit years to discover that the answer is **20**.

Author's Note

I was born in 1974—the same year Ernő Rubik invented his Magic Cube—and was six years old when it was rebranded and landed in America. Of the 200 million Rubik's Cubes sold worldwide between 1980 and 1983, one belonged to me and my brothers. I remember my older brother taking the Cube apart and putting it back together, manipulating the colored stickers, and bragging about being better at solving it than me.

Although I never mastered the Cube the way my brother did, I always had a fondness for puzzles and an admiration for their creators. Four decades later, while working on this book, I felt a kinship with Professor Rubik as I read his memoir *Cubed: The Puzzle of Us All*.

I also bought myself a new Cube. I haven't gotten much better at solving it, but I have a secret weapon now—a young speedcuber in my neighborhood who is more than happy to help. It's a reminder not only of the time that has passed but also of the enduring popularity of the Cube.

As of 2024, more than 450 million Rubik's Cubes have been sold worldwide, and competitions are held regularly around the world to see who can solve one the fastest. In June 2023, Max Park set a new world record by solving the 3x3x3 Cube in just 3.13 seconds. Other feats have included solving it blindfolded, with one hand, or using feet instead of hands. The Rubik's Cube has even been solved underwater, in space, and at the top of Mount Everest!

Learn More

Polinsky, Paige V. *Rubik's Cube Creator: Ernő Rubik*. Minneapolis: Checkerboard Library an imprint of ABDO Publishing Company, 2018.

Rubik, Ernő. *Cubed: The Puzzle of Us All*. New York: Flatiron Books, 2020.

Slocum, Jerry. *The Cube: The Ultimate Guide to the World's Bestselling Puzzle: Secrets, Stories, Solutions*. New York: Black Dog & Leventhal, 2009.

For my family—the invisible core that holds me
together while I twist and turn
—K. A.

Dedicated to Milo K. and his love of solving puzzles
—K. K.

Published by
PEACHTREE PUBLISHING COMPANY INC.
1700 Chattahoochee Avenue
Atlanta, Georgia 30318-2112
PeachtreeBooks.com

Text © 2024 by Kerry Aradhya
Illustrations © 2024 by Kara Kramer

All rights reserved. No part of this publication may be reproduced, stored in a retrieval system,
or transmitted in any form or by any means—electronic, mechanical, photocopy, recording, or any other—
except for brief quotations in printed reviews, without the prior permission of the publisher.

Edited by Kathy Landwehr
Design and composition by Lily Steele
The illustrations were rendered in mixed media and digital collage.
Photo of Ernő Rubik on page 29 © Mike Hollist/ANL/Shutterstock (1524485a)

Printed and bound in January 2024 at R.R. Donnelley, Dongguan, China.
10 9 8 7 6 5 4 3 2 1
First Edition
ISBN: 978-1-68263-664-0

Library of Congress Cataloging-in-Publication Data

Names: Aradhya, Kerry, author. | Kramer, Kara, illustrator.
Title: Erno Rubik and his magic cube / written by Kerry Aradhya ;
illustrated by Kara Kramer.
Description: First edition. | Atlanta : Peachtree, [2024] | Audience: Ages
4–8 | Audience: Grades K–1 | Summary: "This first picture book biography
of Erno Rubik, creator of the Rubik's Cube, reveals the obsession,
imagination, and engineering process behind the creation of a
bestselling puzzle that will celebrate its 50th anniversary in 2024"—
Provided by publisher.
Identifiers: LCCN 2023050584 | ISBN 9781682636640 (hardcover) | ISBN
9781682636787 (ebook)
Subjects: LCSH: Rubik, Ernő—Juvenile literature. | Rubik's Cube—Juvenile
literature. | Inventors—Hungary—Biography—Juvenile literature.
Classification: LCC QA491 .A73 2024 | DDC 793.74 [B]—dc23/eng/20231116
LC record available at *https://lccn.loc.gov/2023050584*

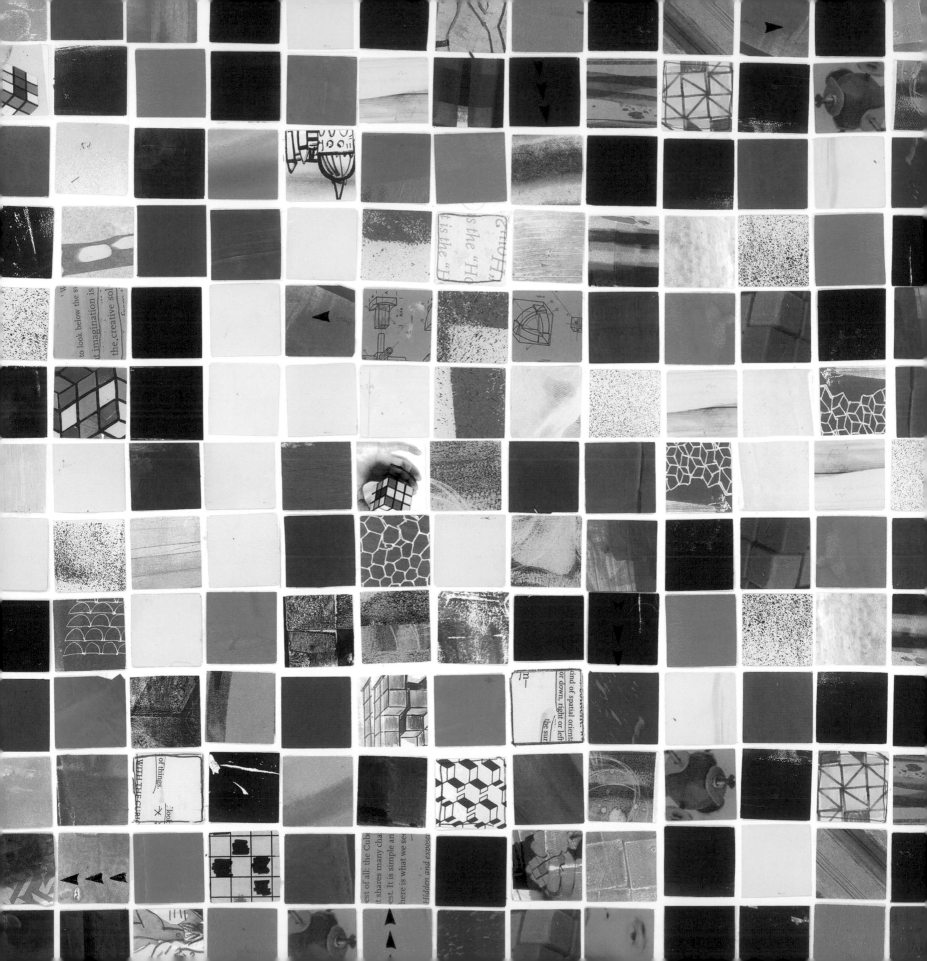